Math Connections

Activities for Grades K-3
Linking Manipulatives and Critical Thinking

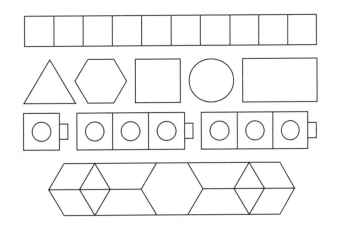

David J. Glatzer

Joyce Glatzer

Dale Seymour Publications®

For Elizabeth—the joy of our lives and our inspiration

Managing Editor: Catherine Anderson
Product Manager: Lois Fowkes
Senior Editor: Jeri Hayes
Project Editors: Suzie Blackaby and Laura Marshall Alavosus
Production/Manufacturing Director: Janet Yearian
Production Coordinators: Barbara Atmore and Joe Conte
Design Manager: Jeff Kelly
Cover Design: Rachel Gage
Text Design: Paula Shuhert

Dale Seymour Publications® is an imprint of Addison Wesley Longman, Inc.

  This book is printed on recycled paper.

ISBN 1-57232-268-3
DS21806

1 2 3 4 5 6 7 8 9 10–ML–00-99 98 97 96

Contents

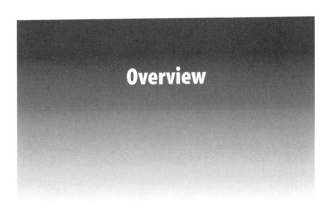

Overview

Manipulatives are powerful teaching tools that can be used by students of all ages but are especially effective for students in the primary grades. Manipulatives allow students to:

- bridge the levels of learning from concrete to representational to abstract
- develop problem-solving strategies
- communicate ideas and insights about mathematics
- become actively involved in the learning process
- use a variety of learning styles
- discover and uncover mathematical relationships
- have fun with mathematics

It is important to note, however, that manipulatives alone cannot be expected to teach a given concept.

In order for students to master a concept that is represented by and explored using manipulatives, you must carefully construct the bridge that will link the activities to the intended mathematical learning. One key way to build that bridge is through thought-provoking questions that cause students to reflect on the activity and determine the connections.

This book offers a variety of teacher-directed activities that are designed to encourage critical thinking, problem solving, reasoning, and communication within the context of the mathematics curriculum. The activities ask students to verbalize understandings of and make connections between key mathematical concepts and hands-on experiences. The activities are intended for grades K–3.

Math Connections includes activities in which students work with the following commonly used manipulatives:

- attribute blocks
- base ten blocks
- interlocking cubes
- pattern blocks

In order for the activities to have maximum value, you will need a sufficient supply of each manipulative. You may want to model the problems, using manipulatives designed for display on an overhead projector. It is assumed but not required that students have had prior experience using these manipulatives. If they haven't, it may be desirable for students to become familiar with the manipulatives through free exploration.

The activities included in this book ask students to build, copy, cover, or complete a wide variety of tasks in order to answer follow-up questions concerning each task. The activities are presented in four parts:

- Which One Doesn't Belong?
- How Do You Know?
- What Happens?
- Same and Different

The activities in each part are linked to key concepts in the K–3 curriculum and offer an expanded set of options to check for understanding.

Format

Each part is divided into lessons that include:

- Curriculum Objective—what is being developed
- Procedure—what students do in the activity
- Making the Connection—the key questions and points that you need to consider in order to help students bridge the understanding between the concrete and the abstract
- Extension—questions or activities designed to challenge students and solidify the key concepts

The way students respond to the questions will vary with their ability to use mathematical language and written form. For example, in early primary grades, responses will typically be presented orally, with students discussing concepts among themselves and with you. As students gain facility with written expression, they can be expected to write their responses, and you may wish to have students keep a math journal. An alternative approach is to have students present a group solution, either in writing or orally, that communicates the conclusions reached by their group. Recommended group size is 2–4 students.

There is no correct or preferred sequence for presenting the material in this book. Select material that supports the math concept you are introducing, developing, or reinforcing.

Suggested Responses are included in the back of the book. It is important to note that these are sample answers. Responses will vary, and you will want follow-up discussion to include the different responses offered by individual students or groups.

Home Link

As you communicate with parents, you might want to give them some idea of the types of questions included in the activities. Parents can be encouraged to ask similar questions in a variety of contexts at home, even if they do not necessarily use the manipulatives. For example, Which One Doesn't Belong? can be used with topics as diverse as money, measurement, geography, sports, and so on.

Consider including the activities found in this book in family math programs that may be conducted in your district.

Introduction

The problems in Part 1, "Which One Doesn't Belong?" allow students to concentrate on the critical attributes associated with specific topics in mathematics. Students are asked to determine how three of four given items are related. The ability to recognize relationships and patterns is fundamental for success in mathematics. Furthermore, the ability to verbalize these relationships facilitates understanding. In stating the rationale for a response, students must indicate the characteristic common to the related items.

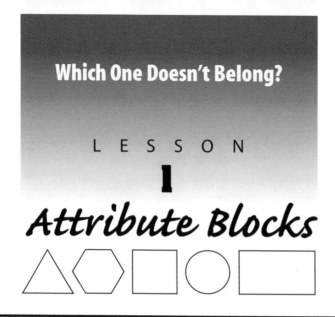

Which One Doesn't Belong?

L E S S O N

1

Attribute Blocks

Curriculum Objectives   Classification and sorting

Procedure

For each problem, pairs of students use attribute blocks to copy each item presented. (Note: Letter abbreviations inside blocks stand for colors.) When students have built all four items for a given problem, ask them which one doesn't belong with the other three. Students should look for relationships among the items. Have students explain their selections. Ask students to identify what the three items share that the one they think doesn't belong seems to lack. Students may suggest more than one correct answer.

**Making the
Connection**

For Problem 2, p. 4, a student might say that item C doesn't belong because the other three items are large and C is small. Another student might say that item B doesn't belong because it is thick. Another might say that D doesn't belong because it is a square. Encourage students to single out as many differences as they can for each question. Students need to be aware that in the attribute set, the pieces are related by size, shape, color, or thickness. The more experience they have working with attribute blocks, the easier it will be for them to see relationships among the pieces.

Extension

Have the students make a booklet that groups the blocks by their attributes. For example, students can draw a picture of the attribute blocks that are square. Point out that all of the blocks they found with this attribute are square, but they also have attributes that make the squares different from each other. Relate this activity to the scientific classification of animals

Which One Doesn't Belong?

1.

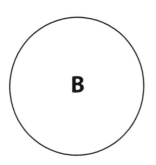

A

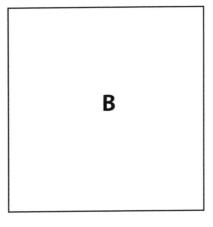

B

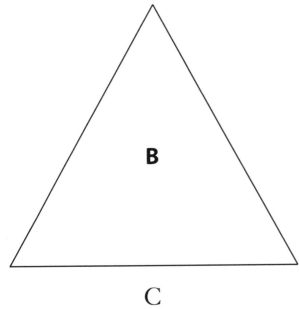

C

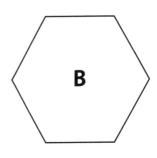

D

Which One Doesn't Belong?

2.

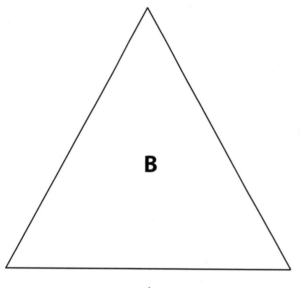

A

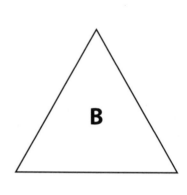

B

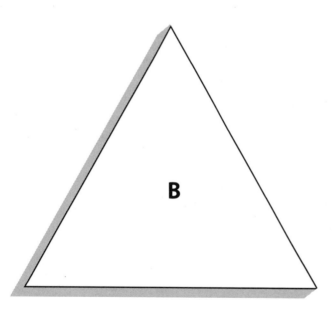

C

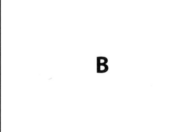

D

Which One Doesn't Belong?

3.

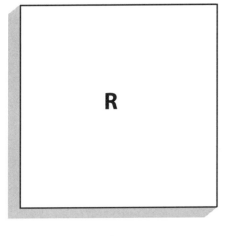

A

B

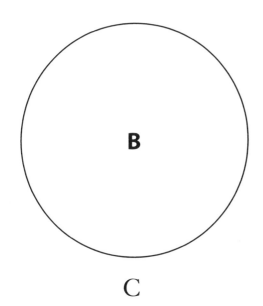

C

D

Which One Doesn't Belong?

4.

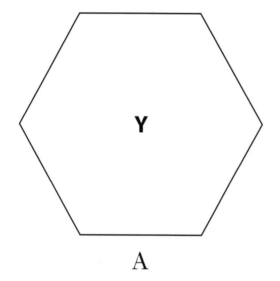

A

B

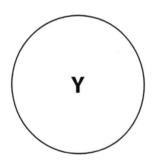

C

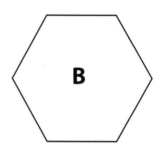

D

Part 1, Lesson 1 • Attribute Blocks

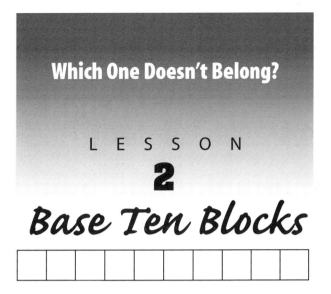

Which One Doesn't Belong?

L E S S O N

2

Base Ten Blocks

Curriculum Objectives   Number representation and place value

Procedure   For each problem, pairs of students use base ten blocks to copy each item presented. When students have built all four items for a given problem, ask them which one doesn't belong with the other three. Students should look for relationships among the items. Have students explain their selections. Ask students to identify what the three items share that the one they think doesn't belong seems to lack. Students may suggest more than one correct answer.

Making the Connection   For Problem 1, on p. 8, a student may say B doesn't belong, since it does not have any single units. Another student might suggest that D doesn't belong, since it has four tens and the others have only three tens. Encourage the students to use the number name to identify each representation. Use this opportunity to reinforce number writing and the relationship of the tens and ones to their position in a digit.

Extension   Have students make up their own "Which One Doesn't Belong?" problems. State a characteristic that must be shared by three of the four items. Students build numbers to satisfy the conditions. Students must explain their selections. For example, have students build three numbers that have two tens in their representation and one that does not. Or have them build three numbers that are greater than ten and one that is less than ten. Student pairs can compare their answers and discuss how the different answers all meet the given conditions.

Which One Doesn't Belong?

1.

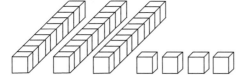

A

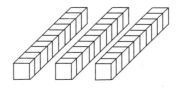

B

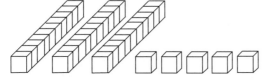

C

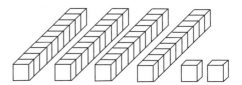

D

Which One Doesn't Belong?

2.

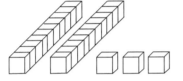

A

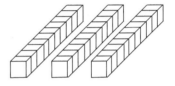

B

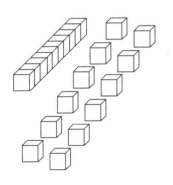

C

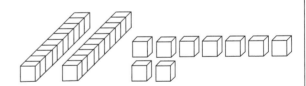

D

Which One Doesn't Belong?

3.

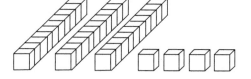

A

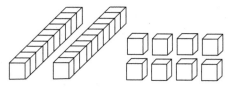

C

B

D

Which One Doesn't Belong?

4.

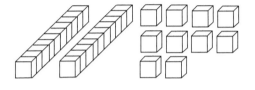

A

B

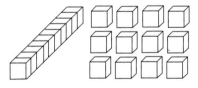

C

D

Which One Doesn't Belong?

5.

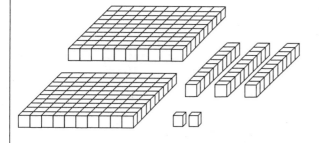

A   B

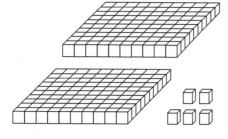

C   D

Which One Doesn't Belong?

6.

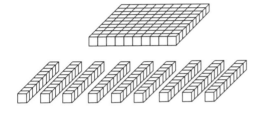

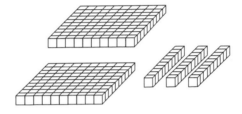

A

B

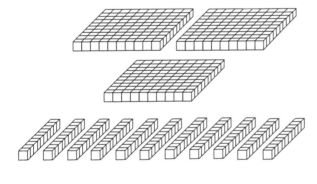

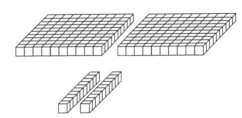

C

D

Name

Which One Doesn't Belong?

7.

A

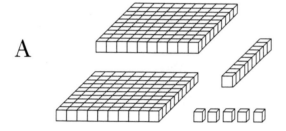

B

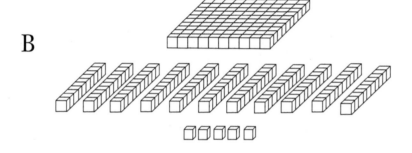

C

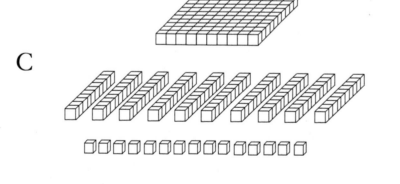

D

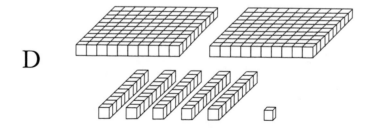

Which One Doesn't Belong?

8.

A

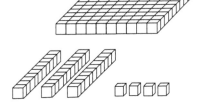

B

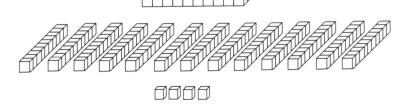

C

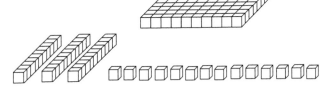

D

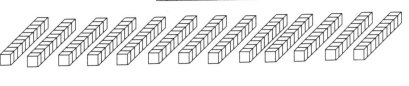

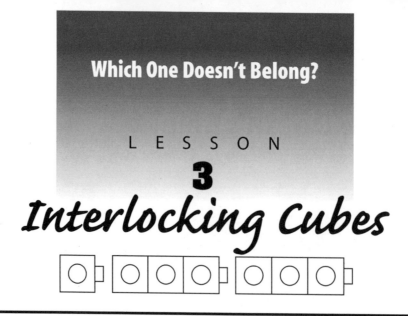

Which One Doesn't Belong?

L E S S O N
3
Interlocking Cubes

Curriculum Objectives   Number sense and patterns

Procedure   For each problem, pairs of students use interlocking cubes to copy each item presented. (Note: Where relevant, letter abbreviations inside cubes stand for colors.) When students have built all four items for a given problem, ask them which one doesn't belong with the other three. Students should look for relationships among the items. Have students explain their selections. Ask students to identify what the three items share that the one they think doesn't belong seems to lack. Students may suggest more than one correct answer.

Making the Connection   For Problem 1, on p. 17, a student might select D because it has the same number of cubes in both rows and the others don't. Another student might select C because the cubes add up to five and the other cubes all add up to six. Encourage students to look for patterns, computational relationships, or spatial relationships. If appropriate, ask students to write number sentences for items that can be related using a computational relationship, as in Problem 1.

Extension   Have students make up their own "Which One Doesn't Belong?" problems. State a characteristic that must be shared by three of the four items. Students build representations to satisfy the conditions. Students must explain their representations. For example, have students build representations in which three of the numbers are doubles and the fourth is not a double. Or have them build three representations that show facts for 10 and one that doesn't. Student pairs can compare their answers and discuss how the different answers all meet the given conditions.

Which One Doesn't Belong?

1.

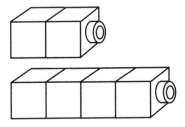

A

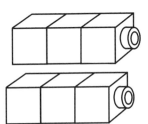

B

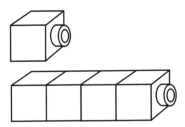

C

D

Which One Doesn't Belong?

2.

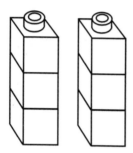

A

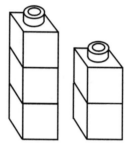

B

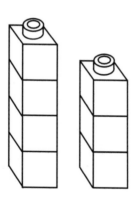

C

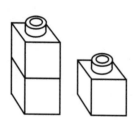

D

Part 1, Lesson 3 • Interlocking Cubes

Which One Doesn't Belong?

3.

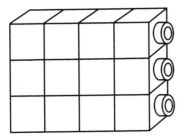

A

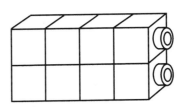

B

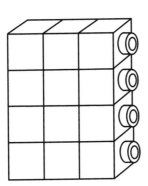

C

D

Which One Doesn't Belong?

4.

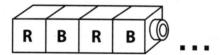

A

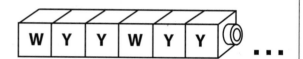

B

C

D

Part 1, Lesson 3 • Interlocking Cubes

Which One Doesn't Belong?

LESSON
4
Pattern Blocks

Curriculum Objectives   Shape recognition, equivalence, and patterns

Procedure   For each problem, pairs of students use pattern blocks to copy each example (A–D) presented. When students have built all four examples for a given problem, ask them which one doesn't belong with the other three. Students should look for relationships among the examples. Have students explain their selections. Ask students to identify what the three examples share that the one they think doesn't belong seems to lack. Students may suggest more than one correct answer.

Making the Connection   For Problem 1, on page 22, a student might select D because it has six sides and the others have only four. Another student might select B because it cannot be covered by green triangles and the other three can. Encourage students to look for equivalent representations for the figures and to suggest other groupings that might display the same idea. The more experience students have working with pattern blocks the easier it will be for them to see relationships and patterns that exist.

Extension   In the set of pattern block pieces, the tan rhombus and the orange square do not have a convenient ratio compared with the other four pieces (blue rhombus, green triangle, yellow hexagon, red trapezoid). Using the green triangle as the unit building piece, have students design two new shapes mathematically related to the other four pieces to replace the tan rhombus and orange square. For example, a parallelogram can be formed using four triangles, or a large triangle can be formed using a red trapezoid and a green triangle.

Which One Doesn't Belong?

1.

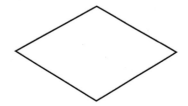

A

B

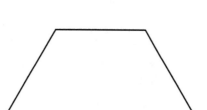

C

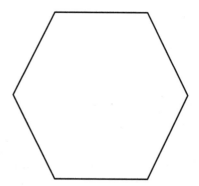

D

Which One Doesn't Belong?

2.

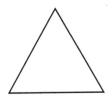

A

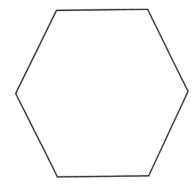

B

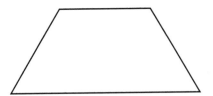

C

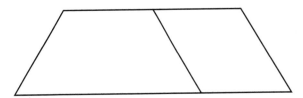

D

Which One Doesn't Belong?

3.

A

B

C

D

Part 1, Lesson 4 • Pattern

Which One Doesn't Belong?

4.

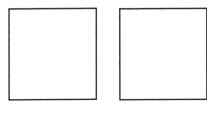

A

B

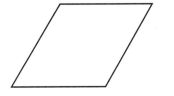

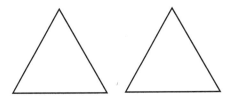

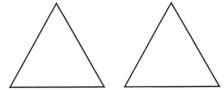

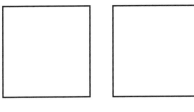

C

D

PART
2

Introduction

The problems in Part 2, "How Do You Know?" give students an opportunity to use words to express key concepts in mathematics. The ability to explain relationships is a better indicator of comprehension than the mechanical completion of standard examples. Therefore, these problems focus on relationships rather than computation. Cooperative learning and divergent thinking are encouraged. Students are challenged to demonstrate number sense by copying or building displays, using the appropriate manipulative for each set of problems. You are provided with a series of questions to ask students, and their responses focus on key concepts.

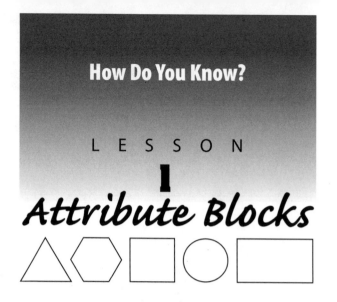

How Do You Know?

L E S S O N

1

Attribute Blocks

Curriculum Objective   Problem solving

Additional Materials   3 loops of yarn per group, index cards

Procedure   Have students arrange two loops of yarn to form intersecting circles, as shown on the student page. Students should write the label indicated on an index card and place it in the circle as shown. Students then place the attribute blocks in the appropriate circles; blocks that share the attributes of both circles are placed in the middle, where the circles overlap. For Problem 3, p. 31, students use three loops of yarn.

Making the Connection   The ability to recognize distinct and shared attributes is the foundation for this activity. To ensure that students understand what they did in Problem 1, p. 30, hold up a red square and ask:

■ How do you know that this attribute block will go in the circle on the right?

Hold up a yellow circle and ask:

■ How do you know that this attribute block will not go in either circle?

Hold up a blue square and ask:

■ How do you know that this attribute block will go where the two circles overlap?

Then ask the following questions:

■ How do you know that only four attribute blocks can go where the two circles overlap?

- How do you know that if the circles are labeled "square" and "circle" there will not be any attribute blocks where the circles overlap?
- How do you know that if the circles are labeled "square" and "not yellow," there will be more than four attribute blocks where the circles overlap?

Extension

For Problem 3, p. 31, arrange three loops of yarn to overlap, as shown on the student extension page. Label each circle with a different attribute. Using labels with negative statements such as "not yellow" or "not circle" increases the difficulty of the activity. Have students sort attribute blocks. Check understanding by asking questions similar to those given in "Making the Connection."

How Do You Know?

1.

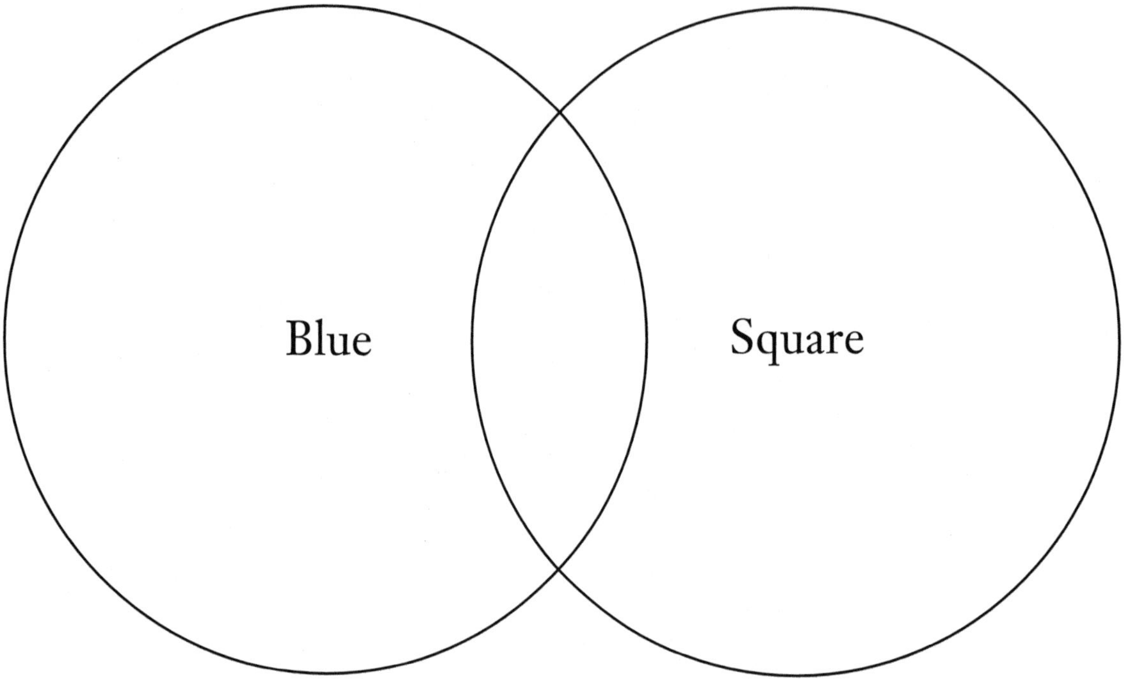

Blue   Square

2.

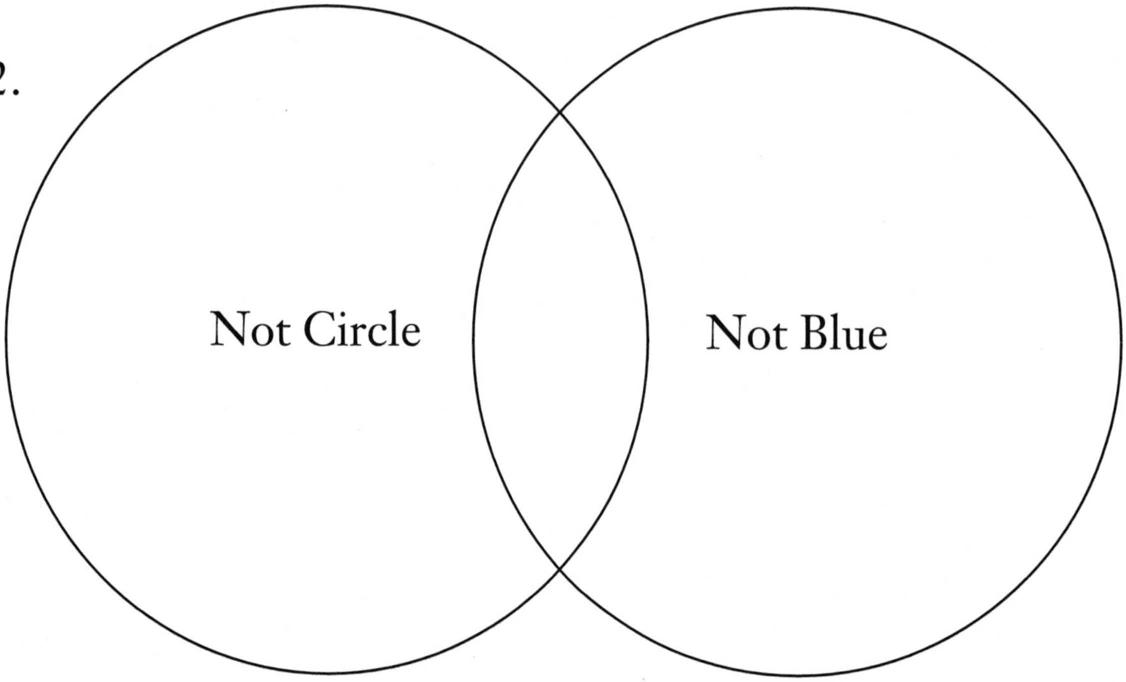

Not Circle   Not Blue

How Do You Know?

3.

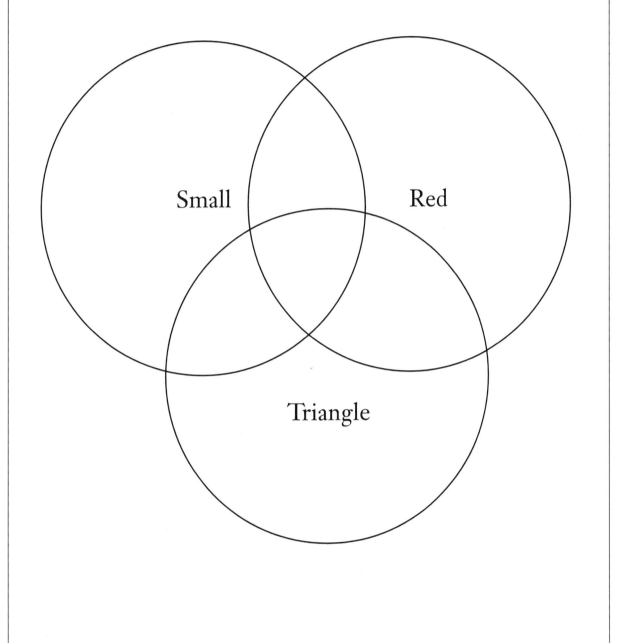

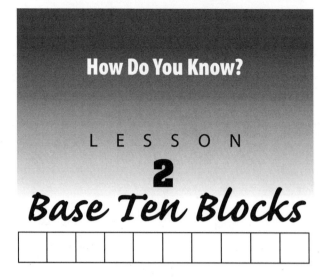

How Do You Know?

L E S S O N

2

Base Ten Blocks

Curriculum Objectives   Number representation and place value

Procedure   Working in pairs, have students build the representations shown for each problem and then name each number. Discuss the number of tens and ones used to build each number.

Making the Connection   Have students look at the representations for A and B on p. 34. Ask:

- How do you know that the number represented in A is larger than the number in B?

An appropriate response might be that while both have 3 tens, the grouping in A has one more unit than the grouping in B.

Have students compare the representations in C and A. Ask:

- How do you know that the number in A is smaller than the number in C?

An appropriate response might be that the representation in A has fewer tens.

Have students compare the representations in D and A. Ask:

- How do you know that the two representations have the same value?

An appropriate response might be that if you regroup the ones in D you will get the same representation as A.

Have students compare the representations in E and A. Ask:

- How do you know that A represents the number that is one greater than the number shown in E?

An appropriate response might be that A has one more single unit than E. If students have progressed beyond tens and ones in place value, hundreds can then be added, as in Problem 2 on p. 35. Ask similar questions for these representations.

Extension

This activity can easily be extended to include the idea of equivalence or the use of other names for numbers. For example, you can ask the students to build a number using as few blocks as possible and then ask questions about the results. Suppose students have used as few blocks as possible to build 43. Ask:

- How do you know that the fewest number of blocks you can use to build 43 is seven?
- How do you know that 43 is the greatest number of blocks you can use to build 43?
- What other ways can you show to make 43?

Similar questions can be asked for any number that you or the students choose.

How Do You Know?

1.

A

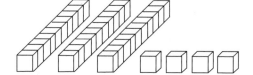

B

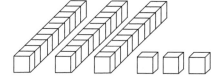

C

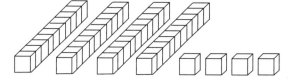

D

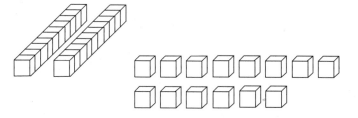

E

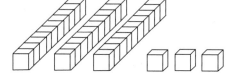

Part 2, Lesson 2 • Base Ten Blocks

How Do You Know?

2.

A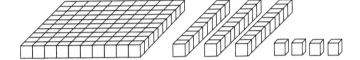

B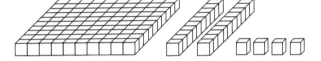

C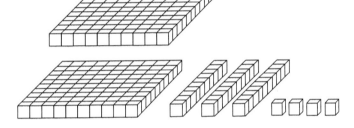

D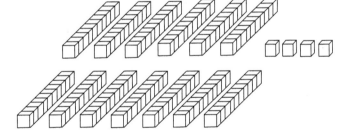

E

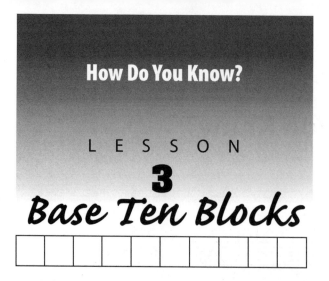

How Do You Know?

L E S S O N

3

Base Ten Blocks

Curriculum Objective   Regrouping

Procedure

Have groups of three students play the game "Give Me." For each round of play, two students exchange cubes; the third student serves as the banker. Following the directions on the sheet, the banker gives Player 1 base ten blocks representing a certain number, using the fewest number of blocks possible. Player 2 then asks Player 1 for a specified number of blocks. Player 1 must either hand over the correct number of blocks or make an exchange at the bank in order to hand over the correct number of blocks. At the end of the round of play, Players 1 and 2 together should have blocks equaling the number that Player 1 had to start with. Players then switch roles and repeat the game.

Making the Connection

It is important that students not only know how to regroup base ten blocks, but also when to regroup them. Ask the following questions to help students focus on knowing when to regroup for Round 1.

- How do you know that if you have 58 you can give away 23 without having to regroup?

- How do you know that if you have 30 you have to regroup to give away 19?

- How do you know that Players 1 and 2 must have a total of 58 blocks at the end of the round?

Ask the following questions to help students focus on knowing when to regroup for Round 2.

- How do you know that if you have 62 you will have to regroup to give away 18?

- How do you know that if you have blocks that value 44 you will have no ones blocks left after you give me blocks with a value of 24?

- How do you know that if the value of the blocks Player 1 has gets smaller, then the value of the blocks Player 2 has must get larger?

Ask the following questions to help students focus on knowing when to regroup for Round 3.

- How do you know that if you have blocks that value 126 and give away blocks that value 15, you will still have a block that values 100?
- How do you know that if you have blocks that value 111 you must regroup to give away blocks that value 23?
- How do you know that Player 1's blocks have a lower value than Player 2's blocks?

Ask the following questions to help students focus on knowing when to regroup for Round 4.

- How do you know that if you have 147 you can give away 23 without having to regroup?
- How do you know that if you have 124 you will have to regroup to give away 19?
- How do you know that if you have 105 you will have to regroup to give away 27?
- How do you know that after you have given away 31 you have given away a total of 100?

Extension

Suppose Player 1 starts with blocks that value 96. Have students write three "Give Me" instructions so that Player 1 gives away blocks without ever having to regroup. Then have them write three "Give Me" instructions that call for Player 1 to regroup for each exchange.

How Do You Know?

Use base ten blocks to play "Give Me." Follow the directions below.

Round One
Player 1 gets blocks that value 58 from the banker.
The banker uses as few blocks as possible.
Player 2 says:
   Give me blocks that value 23.
   Give me blocks that value 5.
   Give me blocks that value 19.
Player 1 Total: _____   Player 2 Total: _____

Round Two
Player 1 gets blocks that value 62 from the banker.
The banker uses as few blocks as possible.
Player 2 says:
   Give me blocks that value 18.
   Give me blocks that value 24.
   Give me blocks that value 11.
Player 1 Total: _____   Player 2 Total: _____

Round Three
Player 1 gets blocks that value 126 from the banker.
The banker uses as few blocks as possible.
Player 2 says:
   Give me blocks that value 15.
   Give me blocks that value 23.
   Give me blocks that value 49.
Player 1 Total: _____   Player 2 Total: _____

Round Four
Player 1 gets blocks that value 147 from the banker.
The banker uses as few blocks as possible.
Player 2 says:
   Give me blocks that value 23.
   Give me blocks that value 19.
   Give me blocks that value 27.
   Give me blocks that value 31.
Player 1 Total: _____   Player 2 Total: _____

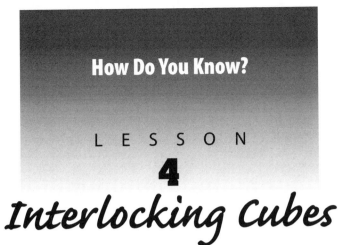

How Do You Know?

LESSON
4
Interlocking Cubes

Curriculum Objective Development of addition facts

Procedure Working in pairs, students use interlocking cubes to build trains 6 blocks long. When building the trains, students may use both red blocks and blue blocks. As they build the trains, students must keep blocks of the same color together. Have students compare their answers. You may have students color in the trains on the problem page if there are not enough cubes to go around.

Making the Connection This problem has students uncover facts for the number 6. The following questions help students use what they know about the number 6 to make generalizations that will help them learn other facts. When students have built all their trains, ask:

- How do you know that there are seven different ways to arrange the blocks?

- How do you know that one possible combination for 6 is 3 red and 3 blue?

- How do you know that if 4 red and 2 blue gives you 6, 2 red and 4 blue also gives you 6?

- How do you know that if there are seven different ways to make 6-block trains, there will be eight different ways to make 7-block trains?

Repeat the problem for trains of different lengths and modify the questions accordingly.

Have students explore ways to make trains of specified lengths using three different colors of cubes. For example, record all the ways you can find to make 4-block trains using red, blue, and yellow blocks. Be sure to keep blocks of the same color together. (There are 15 ways to build three-color 4-block trains.)

Repeat for 5- or 6-block trains.

How Do You Know?

Build trains 6 cars long and place them on the page. You may use red blocks and blue blocks. Keep blocks that are the same color together.

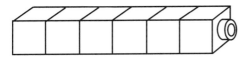

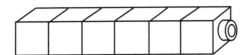

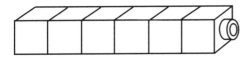

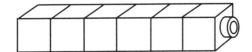

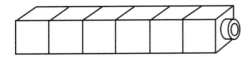

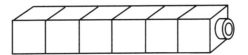

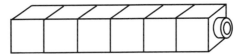

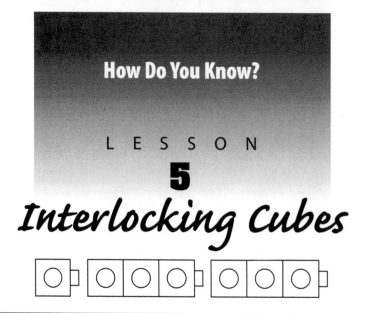

Interlocking Cubes

Curriculum Objectives　Readiness for division, equal shares

Procedure　Students work in pairs to build an 8-block train and then separate the blocks into groups with equal shares, as indicated in the problem. Students record their results in the chart.

Making the Connection　When answering the questions, students will be tempted to say, "Because I did it." This will not help them make the connection between multiplication, skip counting, and division. Therefore, before you ask the given questions, have students review skip counting by the different groups to see when 8 is mentioned. Then ask:

- How do you know that this train can be evenly separated into groups of 2?

- How do you know that this train can be evenly separated into groups of 4?

- How do you know that this train cannot be evenly separated into groups of 3?

- How do you know that this train cannot be evenly separated into groups of 5?

- How do you know that this train can be evenly separated into groups of 1?

- How do you know that this train cannot be evenly separated into groups of 9?

- How do you know that a train that can be evenly separated into groups of 4 can be evenly separated into groups of 2?

- How do you know that a train with an even number of cars can be separated into groups of 2?

■ How do you know that a train of any length can be separated into groups of 1?

Repeat the problem for a train that has a different length and modify the questions.

Extension

An 8-block train can be evenly separated in 4 different ways: groups of 1, 2, 4, and 8. Which trains that are fewer than 20 cars long can be evenly separated into only two groups? (prime numbers: 2, 3, 5, 7, 11, 13, 17, 19) Which trains that are fewer than 20 cars long can be evenly separated into fewer than two groups? (None. Do not consider a train with only one car.)

How Do You Know?

Build a train 8 cars long. Try to separate the train into groups. There should be an equal number of cars in each group. Show your work in the chart.

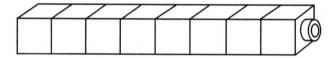

Can you separate the train into even groups of:	Yes/No	If yes, how many groups do you get?
1		
2		
3		
4		
5		
6		
7		
8		

How Do You Know?

L E S S O N

6
Pattern Blocks

Curriculum Objective Mathematical equivalence

Procedure Have students build the figure shown in the problem. After they have built the figure, discuss which blocks they used. Challenge them to build the figure using either fewer blocks or more blocks. Ask them to represent the figure using the fewest number of blocks and the greatest number of blocks.

Making the Connection After students have had sufficient time to explore the figure and try different representations, ask them the following questions.

- How do you know that the fewest number of blocks you can use to build the figure is 6?
- How do you know that the greatest number of blocks you can use to build the figure is 20?
- How do you know that building the figure using only green triangles will take more blocks than building the figure using only blue rhombuses (rhombi)?
- How do you know that this figure can be covered using 10 blocks?

In each case, a response of "because I did it that way" is not sufficient. It is important for students to offer responses that show some understanding of the relationship between the size of the piece used and the number of pieces used. Responses that indicate an understanding of equivalent relationships should be encouraged. This problem provides readiness for understanding the basic fraction concept, "The more pieces a whole contains, the smaller the pieces are."

Extension

Tell the students that they may select any 10 pieces they wish from the red, blue, yellow, or green blocks in the pattern block set. They are to build a design with the 10 blocks they selected. After the design is built, ask them to determine how many green triangles it would take to cover the shape they built. Compare to see which student's design would need the greatest number of green triangles to cover it. Ask students to determine which set of 10 blocks produces a design that needs the greatest number of green triangles to cover it. (10 yellows) Which would need the fewest number of green triangles to cover it? (10 greens)

How Do You Know?

Build the figure.

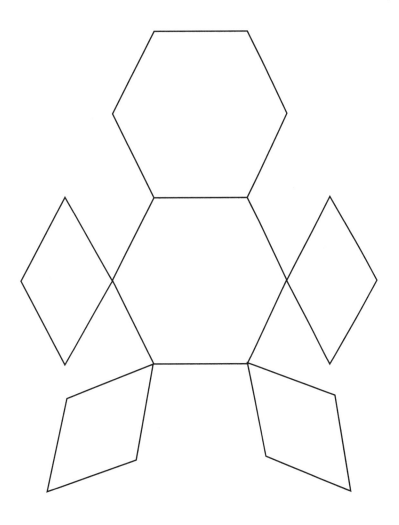

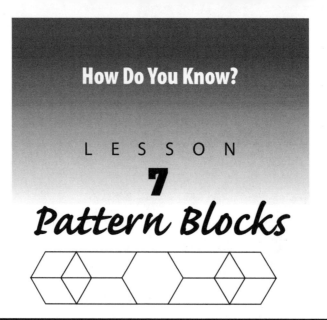

How Do You Know?

L E S S O N

7
Pattern Blocks

Curriculum Objectives Fraction of a region, making congruent figures

Procedure Pairs of students cover the hexagons on the problem page with pieces from the pattern block set. Challenge students to find all seven different ways to cover each hexagon.

Making the Connection If you assign the value of 1 to the hexagon, the red, blue, and green pieces of the set can be given fractional values of 1/2, 1/3, and 1/6, respectively. Students will quickly see that the tan and orange pieces cannot be used to cover the hexagons. To answer the questions, students should focus on the hexagons covered in a single color. The questions will help students make the connections.

■ How do you know that the value of the red trapezoid is 1/2 if the yellow hexagon has a value of 1?

■ How do you know that the value of the blue rhombus is 1/3 if the yellow hexagon has a value of 1?

■ How do you know that the value of the green triangle is 1/6 if the yellow hexagon has a value of 1?

■ How do you know that the value of a block is less if the block is made smaller?

■ How do you know that the value of a blue rhombus and a green triangle together is 1/2 if the yellow hexagon has a value of 1?

■ How do you know that the value of two blue rhombuses is greater than the value of one red trapezoid?

■ How do you know that the value of three green triangles is 1/2 if the yellow hexagon has a value of 1?

■ How do you know that the value of two green triangles is 1/3?

Extension

Suppose you assign two yellow hexagons a combined value of 1. What is the value of the red trapezoid, blue rhombus, and green triangle? Suppose you define the red trapezoid to have a value of 1. What are the values of the yellow, blue, and green pieces?

How Do You Know?

Use pattern blocks to cover each hexagon in a different way.

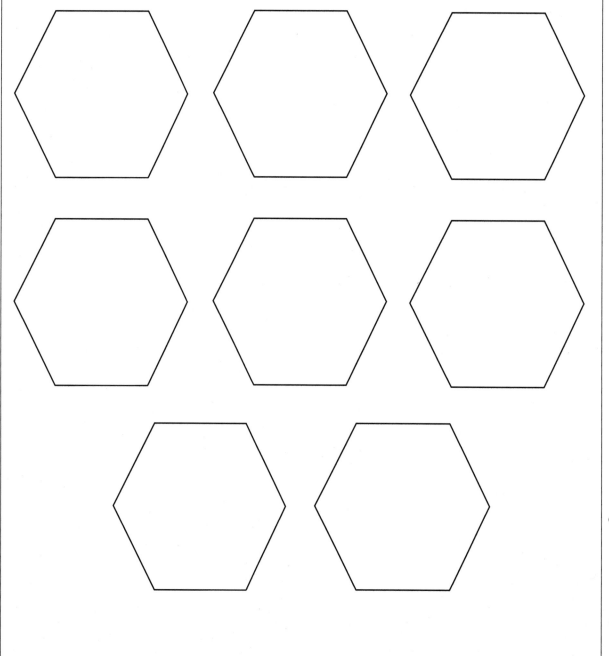

P A R T

3

Introduction

The problems in Part 3, "What Happens?" explore how specific conditions or changes in those conditions impact a situation. Students are asked to determine what will happen if certain changes are made. This activity fosters the development of reasoning skills. Students are expected to discuss or write their responses to the questions. As they formulate their responses, encourage them to examine specific examples that fit the conditions and to use manipulatives or drawings to help them visualize the situation.

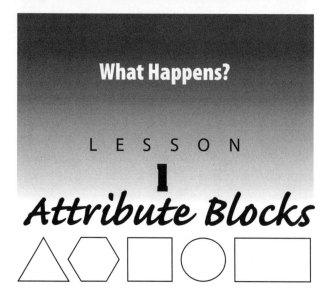

What Happens?

L E S S O N

1

Attribute Blocks

Curriculum Objectives   Classification and sorting

Procedure   Describe the small, thin, red triangle. Have students place it inside the circle on the problem page. Read the "What Happens?" questions one at a time. Students place blocks that satisfy the condition described in the question around the outside of the circle. Have students compare and explain their selections. To repeat the problem, use a different attribute block (large, thick, blue circle; small, thick, yellow rectangle; large, thin, red square) in the circle and ask the questions again.

Making the Connection   The following questions will help students identify common attributes shared by the blocks and will foster a deeper understanding of the objective of classification.

- What if a block differs from the starting block in exactly one way? Which blocks could you put around the circle?

(If this is too hard for younger students, specify how the block differs: color, size, thickness.)

- What if a block differs from the starting block in exactly two ways?

- Which blocks could you put around the circle?

(Again, specify the difference for younger students.)

Extension   After students have placed the blocks around the outside of the circle that differ from the small, thin, red triangle in exactly one way, ask the following questions.

- What if you put the small, thin, yellow triangle in the center of the circle in place of the small, thin, red triangle?

- Which blocks would you have to remove from the outside of the circle?

- Which blocks could you add? What if you changed the starting block to the small, thin, yellow square?

What Happens?

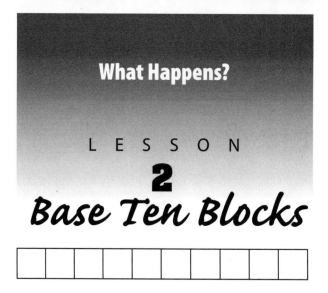

What Happens?

L E S S O N

2

Base Ten Blocks

Curriculum Objectives   Number representation and place value

Procedure   Students work in pairs to build the number specified in the problem, using the number of blocks indicated. Be sure students understand that they are building various representations of the same number. Discuss the difference between the number of the blocks used and the value of the blocks used. For example, three tens and one single unit is four blocks, and they represent the number 31. Four other blocks will represent a different number. Use the questions below to help students reflect on the representations they built and extend their understanding of place value.

Making the Connection   Students should compare and contrast the five different representations for 43. Ask:

- What if you had to represent 43 using the fewest number of blocks possible? Which blocks would you choose?

- What if you had to represent 43 using the largest number of blocks possible? Which blocks would you choose?

- What if you were asked to represent 43 using 10 blocks? Could you build the representation? Why or why not?

- What if you switched the digits in the tens and ones place in 43? What number would you get? Is it larger or smaller than 43?

- What if you switched the tens and ones digits on any number? Will you always get a number that is smaller? Show one number that switches to a larger number and one that stays the same.

Students who can work with hundreds, tens, and ones should complete Problem 2, on p. 57, which has them compare and contrast equivalent representations for 132. Ask:

- What if you had to represent 132 using the fewest number of blocks possible? Which blocks would you choose?

- What if you had to represent 132 using the largest number of blocks possible? Which blocks would you choose?

- What if you exchange a ten for a one? What pattern do you notice?

- What if you switch the digits in the tens and ones place? Would the number be larger than 132?

- What if you wanted to used the digits 3, 2, and 1 once and only once to form the largest three-digit number possible? What number would you get?

- What if you wanted to use the digits 3, 2, and 1 once and only once to form the smallest three-digit number possible? What number would you get?

Extension

Give students different numbers such as 56, 30, or 49. Ask students to find all the different combinations of blocks that can be used to build each number. Ask students to explain the process they used to determine their answers. Relate this activity to finding different ways to express amounts of money using only dimes and pennies. Add other coins to increase the challenge.

What Happens?

1. Build 43 using the number of base ten blocks asked for.

    A. Use only 7 blocks.

    B. Use only 16 blocks.

    C. Use only 25 blocks.

    D. Use only 34 blocks.

    E. Use only 43 blocks.

What Happens?

2. Build 132 using the number of base ten blocks indicated.

A. Use only 6 blocks.

B. Use only 15 blocks.

C. Use only 15 blocks in a different way.

D. Use only 24 blocks.

E. Use only 33 blocks.

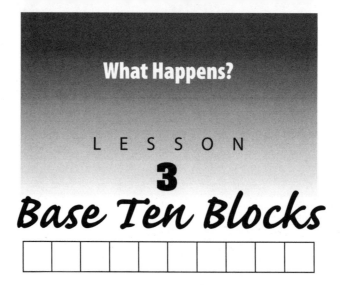

What Happens?

L E S S O N

3

Base Ten Blocks

Curriculum Objective   Regrouping

Procedure   Have students use base ten blocks to represent a given start number—say, 67. Students should represent the number using the fewest number of base ten blocks possible. Read the "What Happens?" questions below and have students add or subtract the appropriate number of base ten blocks to or from their representation and record the value on the problem page. After the questions have been asked, students should record the final number they have. Addition and subtraction statements can be written to represent each action taken. If students have dealt with place value through hundreds, start with a three-digit number—say, 142—for a more challenging activity.

Making the Connection   This activity requires students to use skills in regrouping related to both addition and subtraction. The additions and subtractions should be made using the base ten blocks and then written on the problem page. Begin as follows:

Start with 67.

- Let's begin with 67. What would you have if I gave you 1 ten and 2 ones?

- What if I gave you 1 ten and 6 ones?

- What if I took away 4 tens and 4 ones?

- What if I gave you 3 tens and 9 ones?

- What if I gave you 2 tens and 4 ones?

- What if I took away 3 tens and 8 ones?

For a more challenging activity, present the following questions.

Start with 142.

- Let's begin with 142. What would you have if I gave you 3 tens and 7 ones?

- What if I gave you 2 tens and 1 one?

- What if I took away 4 tens and 3 ones?

- What if I gave you 1 ten and 4 ones?

- What if I gave you 2 hundreds, 3 tens, and 8 ones?

- What if I took away 9 ones?

- What if I took away 2 hundreds, 5 tens, and 8 ones?

Extension

Give students a start number and finish number. Have them write 7 "What Happens?" questions that will get them from start to finish. Have students compare questions. There are many different ways to get from start to finish for any two numbers.

What Happens?

Build the start number using the fewest number of base ten blocks possible.

Show each change in the model by filling in the blank.

I have _____ to start.

Now I have _____ .

Now I have _____ .

Now I have _____ .

Now I have _____ .

Now I have _____ .

Now I have _____ .

I finally have _____ .

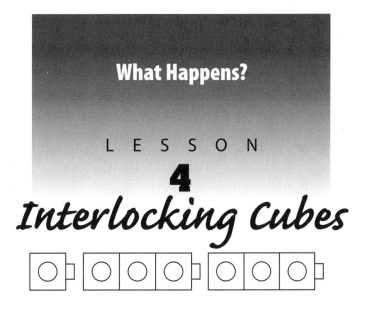

L E S S O N
4
Interlocking Cubes

Curriculum Objectives   Pattern recognition and extension

Procedure   Working in pairs, have students copy and extend each pattern on the problem page using interlocking cubes. (Note: Where relevant, letter abbreviations inside cubes stand for colors.) Ask the students to describe each pattern to their partner. Have them compare the four patterns for similarities and differences. Use the questions provided below to help students better analyze and understand the patterns.

Making the Connection   Recognizing the predictable repetition of a pattern is essential to understanding many important mathematical concepts and relationships. Working with each of the given patterns, ask students the following:

Look at Pattern A.
- What color block will be in the 20th position if this pattern is continued? Can you tell why?
- What letter will be in the 30th position if you put A's on the red blocks and B's on the blue blocks? Can you tell why?
- What color will be in the 20th position if you reverse the positions of the red and blue blocks? Can you tell why?

Look at Pattern B.
- What color block will be in the 20th position if you continue the pattern?

Look at Pattern C.
- What color block will be in the 20th position if you continue the pattern? How does this pattern compare to Pattern B?

Look at Pattern D.

■ What positions in this pattern will have yellow blocks if the pattern is continued for 20 blocks? See if you can find a relationship between the numbers.

■ What positions in the pattern will have red blocks if the pattern is continued for 20 blocks? Describe how these positions are related to the number of yellow blocks.

Extension

What patterns would you form if you had to have green blocks in positions 3, 6, 9, 12, 15, 18 and yellow and/or red in the other positions? Can you rearrange the yellow and red blocks to produce a different pattern that still has green in positions 3, 6, 9, 12, 15, 18?

What Happens?

Use the interlocking cubes to copy and extend each pattern.

A

B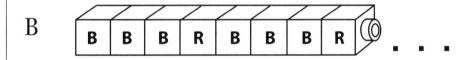

C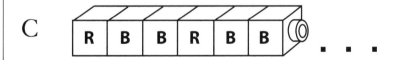

D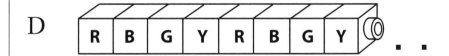

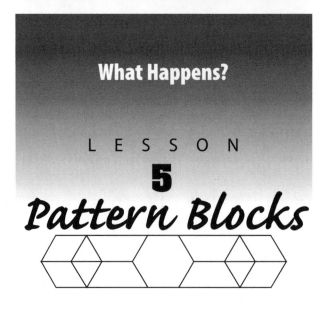

What Happens?

L E S S O N

5

Pattern Blocks

Curriculum Objectives   Meaning of fractions, equivalence

Procedure   Students use the largest pattern blocks possible to cover the design given on the problem page and record the number of blocks in the chart. Students should cover the design three times, first using only red blocks, then using blue blocks, and then using green blocks. Each time the design is covered, students should record the number of blocks used in the chart.

Making the Connection   Students cover the design using smaller blocks each time, so the number of blocks needed increases. Pose the following questions to help students make connections.

- What do you notice happened to the number of blocks needed to cover the design if smaller blocks were used? Explain why.
- What do you notice happened to the number of blocks needed to cover the design if larger blocks were used? Explain why.

Extension   Design your own shape using 7 yellow hexagons. What if you wanted to build the same design using 14 blocks? What blocks would you select? Ask students to state the equivalence relationships between yellow and red, yellow and blue, and yellow and green.

What Happens?

	Yellow	Red	Blue	Green
Number of blocks needed to cover the design				

P A R T
4

Introduction

The "Same and Different" problems in Part 4 provide students with the opportunity to explore the attributes of a given pair of items. Students are expected to analyze each member of the given pair to determine at least one way in which the items are the same and at least one way in which the items are different. Students should be encouraged to state as many common and different attributes of each pair as they can. The activity requires good sense of numbers, relationships, properties, and patterns. While the activity requires use of knowledge and comprehension levels of thinking, students are also challenged to use higher levels such as analysis and synthesis.

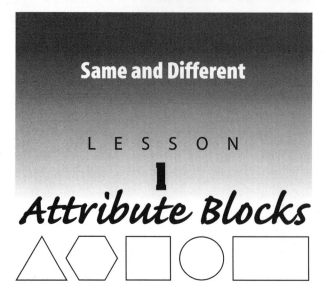

Same and Different

L E S S O N 1

Attribute Blocks

Curriculum Objectives	Classification and sorting
Procedure	Working in pairs, have each student select a block from a bag of attribute blocks and place it in a rectangle on the problem page. Have the students compare their blocks and determine how they are the same and how they are different. Repeat two more times. On the last turn, have the pair of students select three blocks and determine the similarities and differences for the set of three.
Making the Connection	Ask the students to tell you the different attributes or characteristics a set of attribute blocks has, such as shape, size, thickness, color. For each selection, ask the students to state two ways that the two blocks are the same and two ways they are different. Ask if the blocks have more than two similarities and differences. The comparison of three blocks is a higher order activity. Remind students to recall the list of possible attributes (size, shape, color, thickness) when trying to name similarities and differences. This activity can be repeated with material other than attribute blocks. Try using books or collections of pens and pencils.
Extension	Select a block from a set of attribute blocks. Show it to the class. Challenge students to find a block that differs from it in only one way. Have them state the difference. Challenge them to find a block that has only one thing the same as the given block. Have them state the similarity. Repeat the activity, trying for two or more similarities and/or differences.

Same and Different

You and your partner each pick an attribute block from the bag. Place them in the rectangles. How are they similar? How are they different? Do this again. Then repeat, using 3 blocks.

My Block	My Partner's Block

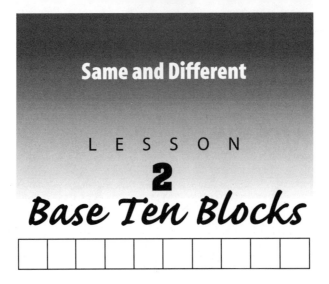

Same and Different

L E S S O N

2

Base Ten Blocks

Curriculum Objectives   Number representation, place value, and comparing numbers

Procedure   For each problem have students work in pairs. One partner uses the base ten blocks to copy the number represented in column A, and the other does the same with the number represented in column B. Ask the pair to compare the two representations, looking for similarities and differences. Be sure students can name the number represented. Problems 6–10, on p. 72, are provided for students who can work with hundreds, tens, and ones.

Making the Connection   Ask the following questions.

- What is at least one thing about the two representations that is the same?

- What is at least one thing about the two representations that is different?

- If you write the numerals for the numbers represented with the blocks, what do you notice that is the same and/or different about their number names?

Have the students change each representation from a base ten representation to one that uses dimes and pennies. Ask them to explain the similarities and differences between the two representations for each amount.

Extension   For each of the given representations on the problem pages, have the students build another representation that has the same attribute that the two given representations share and has the same difference that the two given representations have. For example, in Problem 2, both have 3 tens and different units; students could build 39 as another representation that shares the similarity and difference stated. An example from Problem 5 could have students build 50 and 60 to offer another pair that share the similarity (no units) and the difference (5 tens vs. 6 tens).

Same and Different

Column A	Column B
1.	
2.	
3.	
4.	
5.	

Same and Different

Column A	Column B
6.	
7.	
8.	
9.	
10.	

L E S S O N
3
Interlocking Cubes

Curriculum Objective   Building arrays

Procedure   Using interlocking cubes, have students build the two arrays given on the problem page. Ask students how many cubes were used to build each array. (12) Ask students to identify the shapes of the two arrays. (rectangles)

Making the Connection   The two rectangular arrays pictured have the same area and represent multiplication facts for 12. To ensure that students make the connections, pose the following questions.

- How are the two shapes the same?

- How are the two shapes different?

- Using the same number of cubes, can you make another rectangular shape that is different from the two given shapes? Explain how it is different.

Extension   Using 16 interlocking cubes, have the students build a rectangular array similar to those on the activity sheet. Have the students select another 16 cubes and build another array that is different from the first. Have the students repeat the process until no more arrays can be found. Have students compare the arrays formed using 12 cubes with those formed using 16 cubes. Ask students to list similarities and differences. Note that with 16 cubes, one of the arrays formed is a square. This was not possible with 12 cubes. Similarities will include dimensions used for forming some of the arrays.

Same and Different

Use interlocking cubes to build the shapes below.

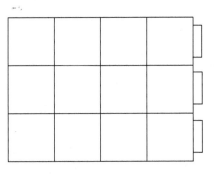

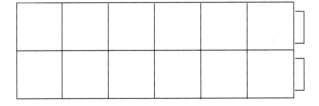

L E S S O N
4
Interlocking Cubes

Curriculum Objective   Finding multiples

Procedure   Have students build 25 pairs of cubes. The cubes in a pair should be the same color, but all pairs need not be the same color. Working with a partner, have students link together the pairs of cubes one at a time. Students begin with a single pair and then link another pair to it and then link another pair to that, and so on. Each time a pair is added on, the length of the resulting train should be determined and that number circled on the chart provided on the problem page. Continue until all pairs have been linked. Then have students build 16 sets of three cubes. In each set the cubes should be the same color, but the different sets can be different colors. Repeat the procedure, linking sets and counting by 3s. Be sure students circle the numbers that represent the lengths formed by linking the sets together.

Making the Connection   Have students compare and contrast the two charts. Ask the students to list any similarities and any differences they see between the two charts. Stress that when counting by 2s you get only even numbers. When counting by 3s, you get some even numbers and some odd numbers. Highlight the numbers that are circled on both charts as an early introduction to common multiples. Discuss patterns that are formed. Use results to develop multiplication facts. Repeat the activity with sets of different lengths. Have students write the resulting multiplication facts in symbolic form.

Extension   Present students with a target number—say, 48. Ask students to determine what size sets of cubes linked together would give a train length of 48. Repeat for other numbers, such as 36, 42, and 60.

Same and Different

A. Count by 2s as you link pairs of blocks. Circle each number as you count it.

1	2	3	4	5	6	7	8	9	10
11	12	13	14	15	16	17	18	19	20
21	22	23	24	25	26	27	28	29	30
31	32	33	34	35	36	37	38	39	40
41	42	43	44	45	46	47	48	49	50

B. Count by 3s as you link sets of blocks. Circle each number as you count it.

1	2	3	4	5	6	7	8	9	10
11	12	13	14	15	16	17	18	19	20
21	22	23	24	25	26	27	28	29	30
31	32	33	34	35	36	37	38	39	40
41	42	43	44	45	46	47	48	49	50

Part 4, Lesson 4 • Interlocking Cubes

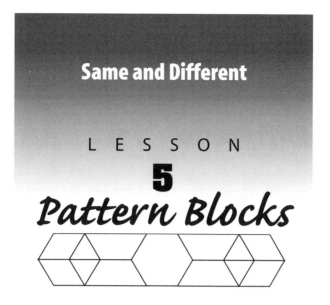

Same and Different

L E S S O N

5

Pattern Blocks

Curriculum Objectives Equivalence, congruent shapes, and problem solving

Procedure Have students work in pairs. Let one student in the pair cover shape A using any collection of pattern blocks he or she wishes to use. When the student has finished covering shape A, have the student tally the number of each type of block used and record it in the chart. Then have the second student in the pair select a different collection of blocks and cover shape B. Have the student tally the number of each type of block used and record the number in the chart.

Making the Connection Ask the students to look at shape A and shape B. It is important that they understand the two shapes are the same. Ask the pair the following questions.

- In which shape did you use the most blocks?
- Can you tell two things that are the same about the way you covered shapes A and B?
- Can you tell two things that are different about the way you covered shapes A and B?
- Do you think it is possible to use the same blocks you used in A but arrange them differently?
- Do you think you can cover the shapes again using a different selection of blocks than were used in A or B?
- Why is it possible to cover the same shape in different ways?

Extension Have the students make a bar graph to show how many of each type of block they used to cover their shapes. Ask them how their graph would change if they exchanged any red blocks used to cover the shape with green blocks. Have them take the same selection of blocks they used to cover their shape and use the blocks to make a different shape. Ask the students how the new shape is related to the original shape. (It has the same area.)

Same and Different

Pick pattern blocks to cover shape A.
Have your partner pick a different collection of pattern blocks to cover shape B.

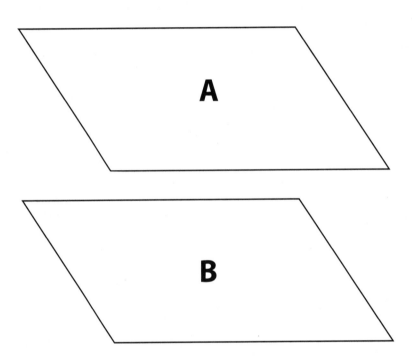

Record the blocks you used to cover each shape.

	Shape A	Shape B
yellow hexagon		
red trapezoid		
blue rhombus		
green triangle		
orange square		
tan rhombus		

Part 4, Lesson 5 ● Pattern Blocks

Suggested Responses

Part 1 Which One Doesn't Belong?   p. 1

Note: In Part 1, please encourage students to say first how three items are similar before saying how the fourth item is unique. For example, in Problem 1, page 3, students should note that items B-D are all polygons (or "have sides") but item A is not.

Lesson 1
Problem 1:   A; because it is a circle.
Problem 2:   B; because it is small.
             C; because it is thick.
             D; because it is a square.
Problem 3:   A; because it is thick.
             C; because it is blue.
             D; because it is small.
Problem 4:   A; because it is large.
             B; because it is thick.
             C; because it is a circle.
             D; because it is blue.

Lesson 2
Problem 1:   B; because it doesn't have single units.
             C; because it is an odd number.
             D; because it has 4 tens.
Problem 2:   B; because it doesn't have single units; it represents 30.
             C; because it can be regrouped.
Problem 3:   C; because it represents 28.
             D; because it is single units.
Problem 4:   B; because it can't be regrouped.
             C; because it has 1 ten.
             D; because it represents an odd number.
Problem 5:   B; because it has only one hundred.
             C; because it doesn't have tens; it represents an odd number.
             D; because it doesn't have single units.
Problem 6:   C; because it can be regrouped.
Problem 7:   D; because it does not represent 215.
Problem 8:   A; because it cannot be regrouped.

Lesson 3
Problem 1:   C; because it isn't a fact for 6.
             D; because it is a double.
Problem 2:   A; because it is an even number.
             D; because it doesn't have 3 cubes.
Problem 3:   D; because it doesn't equal 12.
Problem 4:   B; because it is not an AB pattern.

Lesson 4
Problem 1:   B; because it can't be made from green triangles.
             C; because it does not have equal sides.
             D; because it has more than four sides.
Problem 2:   B; because it can't be covered by an odd number of green triangles.
             D; because it is made from two blocks.
Problem 3:   C; because it doesn't follow the pattern; it has more than one shape.
Problem 4:   A; because it has an odd number of shapes.
             B; because it can't be covered by 6 green triangles.

Part 2 How Do You Know?   p. 27

Lesson 1
Problems 1-3:   Check students' sorting activities.

Lesson 2
Problems 1-2:   Students use representations to make comparisons.

Lesson 3
Round 1:   Player 1 has 11; Player 2 has 47.
Round 2:   Player 1 has 9; Player 2 has 53.
Round 3:   Player 1 has 39; Player 2 has 87.
Round 4:   Player 1 has 47; Player 2 has 100.

Lesson 4

6 blue; 1 red, 5 blue; 2 red, 4 blue; 3 red, 3 blue
4 red, 2 blue; 5 red, 1 blue; 6 red

Lesson 5

An 8-car train can be separated into 8 single units,
four groups of 2, two groups of 4, or 1 group of 8.

Lesson 6

Fewest = 6; Most = 20

Lesson 7

2 red trapezoids
3 blue rhombuses
6 green triangles
3 green triangles, 1 red trapezoid
2 blue rhombuses, 2 green triangles
1 blue rhombus, 1 red trapezoid, 1 green triangle
1 yellow hexagon

Part 3 What Happens?   p. 51

Lesson 1

See Lesson 1.

Lesson 2

Problem 1:   A = 4 tens, 3 single units; B = 3 tens,
             13 single units; C = 2 tens, 23 single
             units; D = 1 ten, 23 single units; E =
             43 single units
Problem 2:   A = 1 hundred, 3 tens, 2 single units;
             B = 1 hundred, 2 tens, 12 single units;
             C = 13 tens, 2 single units;
             D = 12 tens, 12 single units;
             E = 11 tens, 22 single units

Lesson 3

79, 5, 51, 90, 114, 76; 179, 200, 157, 171, 409,
400, 142.

Lesson 4

A. 20th position will be blue; 30th position
   will be B; 20th position will be red if blocks
   in AB pattern are reversed
B. 20th position will be red
C. 20th position will be blue
D. yellow = multiples of 4; red = (multiple of 4) + 1

Lesson 5

7 yellow, 14 red, 21 blue, 42 green

Part 4 Same and Different   p. 67

Lesson 1

Answers will vary depending on which blocks are
chosen for comparison.

Lesson 2

Problem 1:   Both equal 47; B has more tens,
             can be regrouped.
Problem 2:   A = 33, B = 36; both have 3 tens.
Problem 3:   A = 53, B = 33; both have 3 single
             units.
Problem 4:   Both equal 34; both can be
             regrouped; A has more tens.
Problem 5:   A = 30, B = 20; both have only
             tens; A has more tens.
Problem 6:   Both have 1 hundred and 3 tens; B
             has more single units.
Problem 7:   A = 204, B = 240; both have same
             number of blocks, but block values
             are different.
Problem 8:   A = 22, B = 202; both have same
             number of blocks, but block values
             are different.
Problem 9:   Both = 321; B has fewer tens, more
             single units, and can be regrouped.
Problem 10: A = 300, B = 200; both have only
             hundreds; A has more hundreds.

Lesson 3

Same: both are rectangles, both have an area of 12.
Different: one has 3 rows of 4, one has 2 rows of 6;
perimeter = 14, perimeter = 16

Lesson 4

A. multiples of 2
B. multiples of 3

Lesson 5

Answers will vary.